THE LITTLE BOOK OF
Restorative Justice
for
Colleges and Universities

Published titles include:

The Little Book of Restorative Justice by Howard Zehr

The Little Book of Conflict Transformation by John Paul Lederach

The Little Book of Family Group Conferences, New-Zealand Style by Allan MacRae and Howard Zehr

The Little Book of Strategic Peacebuilding by Lisa Schirch

The Little Book of Strategic Negotiation by Jayne Seminare Docherty

The Little Book of Circle Processes by Kay Pranis

The Little Book of Contemplative Photography by Howard Zehr

The Little Book of Restorative Discipline for Schools by Lorraine Stutzman Amstutz and Judy H. Mullet

The Little Book of Trauma Healing by Carolyn Yoder

The Little Book of Biblical Justice by Chris Marshall

The Little Book of Restorative Justice for People in Prison by Barb Toews

El Pequeño Libro De Justicia Restaurativa by Howard Zehr

The Little Book of Cool Tools for Hot Topics by Ron Kraybill and Evelyn Wright

The Little Book of Dialogue for Difficult Subjects by Lisa Schirch and David Campt

The Little Book of Victim Offender Conferencing by Lorraine Stutzman Amstutz

The Little Book of Healthy Organizations by David R. Brubaker and Ruth Hoover Zimmerman

The Little Book of Restorative Justice for Colleges and Universities by David R. Karp

The Little Books of Justice & Peacebuilding present, in highly accessible form, key concepts and practices from the fields of restorative justice, conflict transformation, and peacebuilding. Written by leaders in these fields, they are designed for practitioners, students, and anyone interested in justice, peace, and conflict resolution.

The Little Books of Justice & Peacebuilding series is a cooperative effort between the Center for Justice and Peacebuilding of Eastern Mennonite University (Howard Zehr, Series General Editor) and publisher Good Books (Phyllis Pellman Good, Senior Editor).

THE LITTLE BOOK OF
Restorative Justice
for
Colleges and Universities

Repairing Harm and Rebuilding Trust in Response to Student Misconduct

DAVID R. KARP

Intercourse, PA 17534
800/762-7171
www.GoodBooks.com

Cover photograph by Howard Zehr

Cover Design by Cliff Snyder

Page Design by Mike Bond

THE LITTLE BOOK OF RESTORATIVE JUSTICE FOR COLLEGES AND UNIVERSITIES
Copyright ©2013 by Good Books, Intercourse, PA 17534
International Standard Book Number: 978-1-56148-796-7
Library of Congress Catalog Card Number: 2013937634

Publisher's Cataloging-in-Publication Data

Karp, David R., 1964-
  The little book of restorative justice for colleges and universities : repairing harm
and rebuilding trust in response to student misconduct / David R. Karp.
  p. cm.
  ISBN 978-1-56148-796-7
  Series : The Little books of justice & peacebuilding.

1. Restorative justice. 2. Conflict management. 3. College discipline --United States.
4. Universities and colleges --United States --Administration. I. Series. II. Title.

LB2344 .K37 2013
378.1/95 --dc23   2013937634

Table of Contents

Acknowledgments

Many individuals have helped develop restorative practices for colleges and universities, and I am especially grateful to the following for their leadership, creativity, and advice with this book: Duke Fisher, Sonoo Thadenay, Deb Eerkes, Chris Loschiavo, Josh Bacon, Matt Gregory, Rick Shafer, Nancy Schertzing, Paul Osincup, Stacy Vander Velde, Kevin Mowers, Justine Darling, and Casey Sacks.

Thanks also to Jo Fisher, who, with a keen editorial eye, streamlined the prose and cleaned up grammatical messes. And to Howard Zehr, the Little Books of Justice & Peacebuilding series editor, not only for supporting this project, but for doing so much to spread the word about restorative justice across the planet.

1.
Introduction:
The Story of Spirit Horse

Horse rustling is not the kind of trouble typically caused by college students. But Skidmore College is located in Saratoga Springs, a small city in upstate New York that is known for its high-society thoroughbred racetrack. The population triples in the summertime, and the downtown streets become as bustling and lively as Greenwich Village.

A few years ago, the Saratoga County Arts Council launched a project that decorated the town with life-size fiberglass horses painted by local artists. One of the more interesting horses, called Spirit Horse, appeared to be passing through the large plate-glass window of an antique shop. The statue, cut in half, stood regally on the sidewalk with its rear end inside the store on the other side of the glass. The horse had two glowing green eyes that lit up at night, adding to the spectral mystique.[1]

Late one night, a Skidmore student was returning from the nearby bars and decided he wanted Spirit Horse for his very own. He was able to wrench the front half from its pedestal on the main thoroughfare and was also easily observed by a taxi driver and other witnesses. Police

> *Restorative justice is a collaborative decision-making process that includes victims, offenders, and others who are seeking to hold offenders accountable by having them (a) accept and acknowledge responsibility for their offenses, (b) to the best of their ability, repair the harm they caused to victims and communities, and (c) work to reduce the risk of reoffense by building positive social ties to the community.*

arrived while he was still sweaty and out of breath from hauling it to his second story walk up.

Though this was a minor incident along the continuum of crimes, college administrators were not pleased to read the front page headline, "Skidmore student is charged in theft of decorative horse." They were rightly concerned this would reinforce a community perception of our students as selfish, over-privileged, and a nuisance.

As a restorative facilitator for this case, I was able to host a restorative justice dialogue with the key stakeholders including the student, the artist, the antique shop owner who had paid for the horse, and the arts council director. As is typical of our process, we worked through the case as a campus disciplinary matter before it was handled in the criminal court. There he had been charged with third degree grand larceny and possession of burglary tools—a wrench and pliers.

The beginning of a conference includes storytelling by the offender and each of the harmed parties. The arts council director was surprised to learn, for example, that the student had worked for his hometown's arts council the summer before. With a mixture of remorse and embarrassment, the student revealed that one of his motives in taking the horse was his appreciation for the project and his desire to have a souvenir from it. He quickly added his recognition that this was not the best way to support the arts.

When the restorative justice participants heard from the artist, it was the student's turn to be surprised. The artist described how he had been alerted quite early in the morning after the crime and quickly went downtown to inspect the damage. Of course, he said, he was upset about the theft and damage to his artwork. However, what really upset him were the two live wires that had been ripped from the glowing eyes and left exposed on the sidewalk. He wondered aloud what would have happened had he not been there to remove them. Soon the street would have been filled with toddlers and dog-walkers. Had the student considered that, he asked.

The storytelling in a restorative justice process is designed to explore the harm caused by an offense. In this case, there was property damage and loss but also the risk created by the electrical wires, the community-wide disappointment and anger about vandalism to a public art display, and a spoiling of the reputation of the college.

Once harms are listed, the group works toward solutions that can repair the damage and restore community trust. An agreement was reached in this conference that met everyone's concerns. The student was to be responsible for:

 ✔ Restitution to the artist for costs associated with repairing and reinstalling the horse.

- Restitution to the storeowner based on the cost of sponsoring the horse and the time period the horse was not on display.
- Community service at the Saratoga County Arts Council.
- A daily inspection and cleaning of the repaired "Spirit Horse" for the duration of the exhibit.
- Writing a letter to students moving off campus about being responsible neighbors (to be included in the Skidmore Student Off-Campus Housing Guide).
- Undergoing an alcohol evaluation.
- Organizing an alcohol-free social event on campus.

Impressed by the agreement reached at Skidmore, the Saratoga district attorney negotiated a sentence called "Adjournment in Contemplation of Dismissal." This meant that the student would admit guilt, but as long as he complied with the restorative agreement and stayed out of trouble for six months, his conviction would be sealed, and he would have no permanent criminal record.

About this book

When I facilitated the Spirit Horse case, I was an assistant professor just learning about restorative justice (RJ) and how it was being applied in criminal justice cases around the world. We decided to apply restorative justice principles in this case and discovered the benefits for the student, the harmed parties, and the wider community. Personally, I learned the value of putting an academic interest to the test in a real-world case.

Nearly ten years later, I have continued to examine the use of restorative justice on the college campus through research, teaching, facilitator training and practice, and program implementation. As a student affairs administrator, I have become deeply committed to the concept and practice of restorative justice. I have experienced how it can work given the very real pressures among campus conduct administrators to manage high case loads, ensure fair treatment, minimize institutional liability, protect the campus community, boost morale in a division with high turnover, and help students learn from their mistakes without creating insurmountable obstacles to their future successes.

I wrote this book to encourage colleges and universities to seriously consider implementing restorative practices on their campuses. It is designed to provide an overview of RJ principles and practices, evidence of its effectiveness, and tips on implementation. I provide case examples from a variety of campuses already using RJ, from large public universities to small, private liberal arts colleges.

Having conducted numerous campus RJ trainings, I have seen the need for a short, accessible guide to the topic that can be used as a training manual or stand alone as an introduction for campus decision-makers. Faculty who teach restorative justice may use this as a supplemental text that engages students in a topic of great concern to them—how they may be treated if they get in trouble.

Currently, many people question the value of higher education arguing that it is too expensive, that students are not learning well, and that they are improperly trained to enter the workforce. In the race to cut costs and expand vocational training, institutions often forget to nurture the campus community. The Native American restorative justice practitioner, Ada Pecos Melton, reminds us that "restorative principles refer to the mending process for renewal of damaged personal and communal relationships."[2]

The way we respond to student misconduct symbolizes the kind of community we aspire to be. Just as criminal justice officials have learned they cannot incarcerate their way out of the crime problem, campus conduct officers know they cannot suspend their way out of their student conduct problems. Restorative justice offers a different approach that is educational for the student offender while also meeting the needs of the harmed parties and the institution.

2.
The Principles of Restorative Justice

The Spirit Horse case illustrates four principles that are central to restorative justice.

Inclusive decision-making Restorative justice places decision-making in the hands of the people who care the most—offenders and harmed parties. RJ practitioners provide support and facilitation.	**Active accountability** Restorative justice makes accountability active. Offenders must take responsibility and make amends. They cannot sit back and be judged and sanctioned.
Repairing harm Restorative justice focuses on reparation and healing to bring harmed parties up, not to drag the offender down.	**Rebuilding trust** Restorative justice rebuilds relationships so that offenders can be trusted again and harmed parties can again feel safe.

Inclusive decision-making

Inviting offenders to voice their ideas about how to repair the harm and asking victims and affected community members to articulate the harms they experienced and what needs they have—inviting them all to play a central role in creating a sanctioning agreement—illustrates the first core principle in restorative justice: *inclusive decision-making.*

Sitting in a circle with facilitators who help guide the conversation but who do not offer ideas or solutions of their own, harmed parties and offenders play new and very different roles in the decision-making process than what is common in other campus conduct and judicial processes.

Consider, for example, the roles they play in the criminal courtroom. Defendants have a place to sit, but it is their attorneys who speak on their behalves. Crime victims have no place except as observers in the gallery. And for witnesses, even the observer role is denied.

The most dissonant role in the courtroom is that of defendants, nearly asleep at their own trials, with nothing to do and little understanding of the technical language that is being spoken, which is so decisive regarding their fates. In the restorative process, the student offender, the artist, the storeowner, and the arts director are not marginalized observers, but central actors in the drama of decision-making.

On college and university campuses, the standard disciplinary process is typically offender-centric. Most often, a single conduct officer will meet with the student, discuss the incident, and decide on the spot what the sanction will be. Sometimes a conduct board will listen to the facts as presented by the offender and a complainant, but the board will send them to a waiting room while it privately deliberates about the sanctions. Offenders and harmed parties do not have a strong voice in this process.

Because the artist, storeowner, and arts director are not members of the campus community, it is not likely that they would have been invited to participate or even hear about the outcome of the Spirit Horse case. They would not have learned of the campus's concern about the incident, and they would not learn anything about the student that might offset the negative stereotypes promoted in the local newspaper. They would not have been able to share the varied ways in which they were impacted by the incident and what needs and concerns they had after what happened.

Active accountability

Secondly, restorative justice focuses on *active accountability*. Offenders must take active responsibility for their transgressions. Often, in our criminal justice or campus conduct proceedings, offenders are able to distance themselves emotionally and remain quite passive.

The archetypal image is a young man sinking down in his chair with his arms crossed against his chest and a baseball cap pulled low over his brow. It is as if his body is saying, "I'm not here. You can't reach me." Even if he has admitted responsibility, often he will say, "Yes, I did it. I didn't mean it. Just tell me what you want me to do so I can get out of here."

The storytelling process is a direct challenge to this passive position. It is much harder to ignore the artist, shopkeeper, and arts director who are sharing real experiences and emotions and seeking to make eye contact with the offender, drawing him outside of himself and into a larger, communal understanding of the incident and its consequences.

> *"This process, which I will refer to here as earned redemption, requires a sanctioning approach that allows offenders to make amends to those they have harmed to earn their way back into the trust of the community."[3]*
>
> Gordon Bazemore
> Professor of Criminal Justice
> Florida Atlantic University

A restorative facilitator asks the offender, "Now that we have identified the harms, what can you do to make things right?" This question signals the importance of the offender's active participation. Even if the first answer is "I don't know" or "whatever you tell me to," the facilitator's role is to continue to invite participation by probing and eliciting ideas.

It is with this process that offenders come to own the sanctions as their own, with their ideas included and their spoken commitment. This not only increases the likelihood that they will follow through, but also that they will not reject the sanctioning tasks as coercively imposed or arbitrary.

Repairing harm

A third core principle in restorative justice is the focus on *repairing harm*. Restorative justice is guided by the question, "How can the victim and the community be restored?" Traditional or retributive justice is guided by one that asks, "How should the offender be punished?"

In a sense, both questions respond to the symbolism of Lady Justice holding her scales. The crime has thrown the scales out of balance, and Lady Justice must right them. But the intentions are quite different—one is for repair and is victim-centered; the other is towards punishment and is offender-centered. Retributive justice wants to know what the college will do *to* the student to match the harm he caused to Spirit Horse and the community. Restorative justice wants to know what the college will ask of the student to make things right.

> *"Restorative dialogue... [is where] the problem rather than the person is put in the center of the circle."*[4]
>
> John Braithwaite
> Law Professor, Australian National University
>
> Declan Roche
> Law Professor, London School of Economics

It may, in the end, be challenging or difficult or unpleasant for the offender to make amends, but this suffering is not the goal and is avoided, if possible. Instead, the goal is to do what can be done to undo the damage and return the community to a state of well-being.

How can the student contribute to the restoration and upkeep of Spirit Horse? How can he support the arts council? How can he improve relations between off-campus students and their neighbors? How can he encourage other students to avoid binge drinking and the poor judgments that go along with it? It is these questions that led to restitution, community service, a new off-campus housing guide, and organizing an alcohol-free social event as reparative tasks.

Rebuilding trust

Beyond repairing harm, a final core principle is included in restorative justice. This is to *rebuild trust*. The offending behavior naturally generates mistrust and hesitation about the status and inclusion of the offender in the community. The simplest and most tempting response is banishment from the community: imprisonment in the criminal justice system and suspension from campus.

In restorative justice, we seek to rebuild relationships between distrusting parties not because it is a "touchy-feely" solution, but because it is necessary for stable community and often for the well-being of the victim. Because an offender has abrogated community trust, it is part of his or her obligation to renew it. Because trust is not quickly regained, the process requires a conferencing process that fosters dialogue and mutual understanding and then clearly articulated tasks and benchmarks that build confidence in the community as they are achieved.

In Saratoga, the harmed parties were naturally wary of the horse thief's behavior, and they questioned him closely about his drinking. To help restore their confidence in him, the student agreed to participate in an alcohol evaluation and follow any recommendations from it.

It was a notable moment during the Spirit Horse case when the arts council director invited the student to do community service in her agency. Rather than moving in the direction of suspension, the conferencing dialogue enabled her to see the student as a multidimensional person—flawed in some areas but having strengths in others. With this nuanced perception, she saw how he could make a genuine contribution to her public arts projects, repairing the harm but also building positive relationships in the community.

Grounding a disciplinary response in these four RJ principles helps support student development by teaching students how to take responsibility for their misbehavior actively and productively. While most colleges and universities provide their students with clear conduct policies, they rarely articulate their punishment philosophy. In the next chapter, we will examine how restorative principles can be incorporated into campus codes of conduct.

3.
Restorative Justice in the Model Student Conduct Code

At the University of California-Santa Barbara, some students were entertaining themselves in their residence hall lounge by binge drinking and lighting their leg hairs on fire.[5] One of the students, "Steve," accidently lit the upholstered arm of his chair on fire. While stamping it out, he got carried away and proceeded to demolish several pieces of furniture. The damage was estimated to be over $500, subjecting Steve to felony vandalism charges as well as campus disciplinary review.

Model conduct codes

Without knowing much about Steve, it is easy to ponder sanctions proportionate to the offense. We might, for example, place Steve on probation, ask him to pay restitution, and suspend him from the residence hall. Most conduct administrators write their disciplinary policies based on model codes of student conduct published by national leaders in the field such as Gary Pavela[6] as well as Edward Stoner and John Lowery.[7] These model codes enumerate a typical list of potential sanctions: warning, probation, loss of privileges, fines, restitution, residence hall suspension, academic suspension, expulsion.

While these sanctions are commonplace, we rarely examine the underlying philosophy behind them. Notably, this is a model of progressive exclusion. As the offense becomes more severe, the strategy is to further separate the student from the institution. This makes perfect sense if the goal is simply to protect the campus community from further harm or risk, but most conduct offices also have a goal of helping students learn from their mistakes. Indeed, the Council for the Advancement of Standards in Higher Education argues that "Student Conduct Programs in higher education must enhance overall educational experiences by incorporating student learning and development outcomes in their mission."[8]

"Student conduct officers are not employed to find new and more efficient ways to dismiss students. One of our primary roles—recognizing that dismissals are sometimes necessary—is to help students who commit disciplinary offenses make amends and stay enrolled. That goal requires keeping a fresh and open mind to creative educational strategies."[9]

Gary Pavela
Director of Academic Integrity, Syracuse University

Conduct processes as education

Learning in student conduct often comes in two forms. First, Steve could learn that his behavior was morally wrong because it was harmful to the community. Second, he could learn that membership in a community implies a social contract and there are costs to nonconformity. The first has to do with a *moral* actor, one who considers whether an act is right or wrong. It assumes Steve can feel the pangs of conscience. The second refers to a *rational* actor, one who calculates risk and reward, costs and benefits. A conduct process can address both, but an educational process should always begin with a moral dialogue.

> An educational process should always begin with a moral dialogue.

A discussion of harm is inherently a moral dialogue because it focuses on the impact of the behavior on others. We would call a person who simply does not care about others amoral. It is not unusual for offenders to have tunnel vision, focusing solely on themselves in a self-interested way. Calling attention to the harm through restorative practices redirects their attention, eliciting empathy and conscience. Most often, offenders "get it," feel remorseful, and are then ready to take responsibility by trying to make amends.

This is the ideal outcome in a conduct case because all parties may be reassured that the offender shares the same moral standards and only needed to be reminded of them. Steve participated in an RJ conference and learned about the impact of his actions on an understaffed maintenance crew, how he had betrayed the trust of a residential life staff member who had stood up for him in the past, and how he had disappointed and worried his mother about his drinking and his ability to successfully complete college.

Limits to restorative approaches

Unfortunately, restorative practices do not always work and are not meant to replace other approaches. Instead, they are meant to precede them with the hope that other approaches will not be necessary. Some offenders are simply too self-consumed to care about the impact of their behavior on others. Failing to appeal to their conscience, we must appeal to their rationality. "Even if you do not care about this rule and the consequences of your behavior on others, you should recognize the cost of your behavior on yourself."

Deterrence is the overarching philosophy here. Rational offenders are deterred from future misbehavior because they do not enjoy getting caught and suffering the penalty. They analyze the risk and the costs and decide that causing more offense is not worth the trouble. Deterrence-based sanctions may be effective, but the outcome is less ideal than with restorative sanctions because they do not cultivate moral engagement. Without a moral foundation, if the incentives change, the misconduct may return.

> **Without a moral foundation, the misconduct may return.**

If the offender is neither moral nor rational, we are in deeper trouble. Such offenders are immune to moral appeals and rational disincentives. Fortunately, there are not many such individuals. It is for this group that we must respond with incapacitation, coercively stopping them from further offending. On the college campus, this generally means suspension or dismissal—removing them from the community either temporarily or permanently.

A sanctioning pyramid

Although it is common to pit one type of sanction against another, the sanctioning pyramid[10] suggests they can be complementary. One can be used for moral dialogue, another to establish proper disincentives, and a third as a last resort.

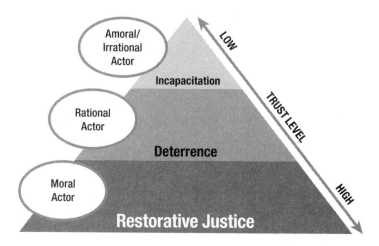

The pyramid encourages us to begin with a sanctioning approach that cultivates internal social controls or self-regulation. We want students to be guided by conscience, able to consider the long term consequences of their actions for themselves and others. We also begin with restorative responses because this approach offers the most decision-making control to the core stakeholders. Harmed parties have a voice in the outcome. Offenders are more likely to take ownership because they are part of the decision.

Offenders are more likely to take ownership when they are part of the decision.

Consider the kinds of sanctions that emerged from Steve's RJ conference. He was asked to pay for the damage to the furniture and volunteer to work with the maintenance crew. Because of the group's concern about his alcohol use, he agreed to attend thirty Alcoholics Anonymous meetings. Because of his betrayal of trust with his resident assistant, the two agreed to work together on floor programming. Rather than distance Steve further from the campus community, these responses helped to strengthen his ties to the community by building positive relationships and strong mentoring opportunities.

While the sanctioning pyramid suggests that RJ and model conduct codes are complementary, it is important to distinguish them clearly.[11] Most importantly, traditional model code hearings are best used when accused students deny responsibility. Similar to the criminal court, model code hearings are carefully orchestrated to maintain civility, respectability, and fairness while board members listen to two opposing sides present evidence and counter-evidence. Complainants, respondents, witnesses, and advisors all have carefully prescribed roles. The primary goal is to determine if the accused student violated the student code of conduct,

and board members undertake this in private delibera-
tion. Sanctions, generally selected from a short menu of
options, progressively limit membership from the campus community.

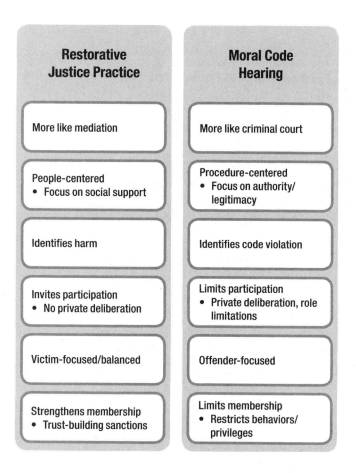

Restorative Justice Practice	Moral Code Hearing
More like mediation	More like criminal court
People-centered • Focus on social support	Procedure-centered • Focus on authority/ legitimacy
Identifies harm	Identifies code violation
Invites participation • No private deliberation	Limits participation • Private deliberation, role limitations
Victim-focused/balanced	Offender-focused
Strengthens membership • Trust-building sanctions	Limits membership • Restricts behaviors/ privileges

Restorative justice assumes that the accused student has admitted fault, which quickly shifts the focus

toward the future—what can be done to make things right. Less attention is paid to procedures than to the participants and manifesting an authentic and engaged dialogue. The goals are to have the parties gain a deeper understanding of one another, acknowledge the harm caused by the offense, repair the damage to the extent possible, and strengthen the students' relationships with each other and with the institution.

Model codes of student conduct allow for the use of restorative sanctions because they include a general category called "discretionary sanctions" or "other sanctions." Of course, any institution can revise its code of conduct to highlight restorative options rather than hide them inside a generic category. In addition to outlining potential sanctions, codes of conduct also describe disciplinary procedures and in the next chapter, I outline three restorative justice practices. While they all have RJ principles in common, each provides a different procedure or approach to fulfilling RJ goals.

4.
Three Models of Campus Practice

R estorative justice is a global movement with practices that have unique histories but borrow and
blend as they evolve. Practices have emerged from contemporary criminal justice systems, faith-based communities, academia, and indigenous justice practices
from Canada to New Zealand. The RJ pioneer, Dennis
Maloney, once said, "Restorative justice is an ancient
idea whose time has come."[12]

As campuses begin to explore restorative justice, they borrow from various traditions and styles of practice. At the core of every practice, however, is a facilitated dialogue between offenders and harmed parties to identify the harm that was caused and how it can be repaired, including the goal of rebuilding trust.

While RJ practices share a common set of goals, three distinct practices are being implemented on college campuses: conferences, circles, and boards.

Restorative justice conferences

This model focuses on the facilitated dialogue between the offender and harmed parties. After discussing the harm, the parties (instead of a hearing officer or conduct board) decide what steps the offender can take to repair the harm. Trained facilitators guide the dialogue.

> *"Conferencing is an opportunity for students who are referred to the conduct office to have a chance to meet face to face with the individuals they have impacted, take responsibility, make amends, build relationships, and move forward in a positive way through support from the campus community."[13]*
>
> Justine Darling
> Restorative Justice Coordinator
> University of San Diego

At the University of San Diego (USD), a Catholic university with more than 8,000 students, RJ conferencing began as collaboration between the Office of Student Conduct and the USD Joan B. Kroc School of Peace

Studies. RJ conferences are hosted by trained facilitators, who use a script to guide the flow of dialogue (see Chapter 12). Prior to the conference, the facilitator meets with the parties involved to educate them about the program and learn about the details of the case.

Like the University of San Diego, Michigan State University also uses restorative conferencing. The Department of Student Life at MSU handles conduct issues and received a complaint that "Henry" had disrupted a final exam when he entered the classroom to retrieve a personal item, was asked to leave, and then became belligerent. A hearing officer met with Henry to explain the conduct process and decide if this would be a good case to refer to RJ. Hearing Henry admit to the misconduct, the hearing officer suggested that he try the RJ process as an interim step before proceeding to a conduct hearing. If successful, the conduct hearing might no longer be necessary. When Henry agreed, the hearing officer referred the case to the RJ facilitator or co-facilitator team.

Once the RJ facilitator receives a referral, the next step is to determine who should participate in the RJ conference. In this instance, harmed parties included the students who were taking the exam, the proctor who told Henry to leave the classroom, and the professor for the course. During the pre-conference meetings, the facilitator learned that the proctor wished to participate but would be unable to attend because she would be at an internship several hours away. The facilitator had to choose between excluding the proctor, having the proctor write an impact statement to be read at the conference, re-scheduling, or having the proctor participate by phone or Skype. Working with the proctor, they decided that a telephone conference call would work best.

During the conference, Henry was able to take responsibility for his behavior and express his remorse. The harmed parties were able to share exactly how they were impacted. For example, they explained that a number of students submitted incomplete exams, stating that the disruptions had made it hard for them to finish on time. One student, who did finish on time, said it had been difficult to concentrate, and she didn't do as well as she could have. Afterwards, the professor allowed students to complete a make-up exam, which was an extra burden for both the students and the department.

Once the harmed parties shared, the participants agreed to have Henry write a letter of apology to the students who had been taking the final exam. The faculty member would distribute the letter (without Henry's name because of confidentiality concerns), believing it was an important way to show that the department took action and held the student accountable. The faculty member also agreed to withdraw the complaint after the apology letter was received, so that a conduct hearing would not be necessary.

Soon after the conference, Henry submitted a draft of the apology letter to the facilitator, who used this as an opportunity to provide guidance and support and to make sure that the letter was well-written and would be well-received by the harmed parties. Students in the class let the faculty member know that they appreciated the letter. Because the case was handled informally, the student was able to avoid a conduct hearing and a permanent disciplinary record.

Restorative justice circles

RJ circles are similar to RJ conferences but often involve a larger number of people and borrow practices from indigenous traditions, especially the Native American practice of using a "talking piece." This is a symbolic or sacred object that is held by the speaker, indicating that no one else should speak. The talking piece is passed around the circle, creating a unique rhythm of dialogue. At James Madison University in Virginia, a JMU centennial medallion is used because it symbolizes the values and culture of the institution—its one hundred year history and the pursuit of liberal learning. The talking piece becomes a reminder of their common values and purpose.

Circle practices may have a spiritual dimension to them, sometimes drawing directly on indigenous rituals and stories or the particular culture or faith of an institution. Christian schools, like Liberty University in Virginia, sometimes incorporate prayer into their circles. JMU, a secular public university, draws upon the "Madison Way," a set of eight principles that guides membership in the campus community: scholarly, honest, studious, accountable, respectful, resilient, compassionate, and invigorating. In addition to the talking piece, JMU includes a copy of the Madison Way as a centerpiece in the middle of the circle, and the facilitator or "circle keeper" talks about it as part of the introduction.

Four rounds

The facilitator is responsible for setting a tone of respect, hope, and support. Circles tend to be organized in four "rounds," with the talking piece making its way around the circle once per round.

During the *first* introductory round, the facilitator welcomes the group and summarizes the issue that brought everyone together. Participants introduce themselves, explain why they are present, and what they hope to achieve from the process. The circle keeper summarizes the hopes expressed.

"At James Madison University, the restorative practice we use the most is the circle process. We have found the key to a successful restorative circle is the pre-circle work. This includes meetings with the harmed party, the party that caused the harm, community stakeholders, and co-facilitators. We use the circle process not only for issues where harm has been done, but to build community in various groups, organizations, and teams (including residence halls, athletic teams, fraternities and sororities, and leadership groups). Many people have commented at the end of a circle process how easy it was for the facilitator and how the facilitator barely did anything. This couldn't be farther from the truth; the facilitator is responsible for the pre-circle work, introducing the process and the guidelines, and facilitating dialogue that respectfully addresses the harms, needs, and obligations of all circle participants. A good facilitator will be not only listening, but watching non-verbal communication in order to determine how to proceed."[14]

Josh Bacon
Director of Judicial Affairs, James Madison University

In the *second* round, participants share their feelings and perceptions about the issue, identifying aspects that are important to them. The facilitator summarizes key emerging themes, areas of agreement and disagreement, and the harm that has been identified.

During the *third* round, participants share ideas about what needs to happen for resolution to occur.

Finally, the closing round enables participants to offer final comments or observations about what the circle meant to them.

In addition to conduct cases, circles are often used for disputes, such as fights where the line is blurred between who is an offender and who is a harmed party. Circles are also used for incidents where there is no offender or the offender has not been identified, but harmed parties want to share their concerns, find support, and/or create plans for the future. A powerful example of using a circle process was at the University of Vermont after a student committed suicide. According to Residence Life Director Stacy Miller, "We couldn't have known when we started doing community circles that a tragedy like this would occur....But since we were already doing the circles, when a crisis hit we knew exactly what to do.... The process has given our students a voice; a voice to share how they feel, heal, and move forward together."[15]

Restorative justice boards

Restorative justice boards have the structure of a "model code" conduct board with standing board members who may be drawn from faculty, staff, and students. However, they are run more like an RJ conference than a model code hearing. Harmed parties are invited but are not needed for the board to proceed. While RJ boards retain the ability to have private deliberations and make their own determinations about sanctions, these practices are avoided to increase the active participation of offenders and harmed parties.

Skidmore College has been operating an RJ board since 2000. The clear advantage of this model is that all conduct cases may be referred to the board, whereas other RJ practices are careful to limit RJ referrals to cases where a harmed party is willing to participate. When a harmed party declines, then board members will represent his or her perspective, often by reading an impact statement.

More broadly, board members serve as representatives of the community and speak to the harm caused indirectly, such as how the student may have tarnished the reputation of the institution. When the case is adversarial—the offender is denying responsibility—the board operates initially very similarly to a model code hearing by reviewing the evidence and making a determination. However, during the sanctioning portion of the board process, the decision-making is focused on the key RJ goals of *repairing harm* and *rebuilding trust*.

While boards offer gains in efficiency, they do have some disadvantages. Some of the emotional immediacy of conferencing and circles is lost by having several participants (board members) who were not directly involved in the incident. Without a direct connection, board members can start to treat cases in a routine or formulaic manner, almost jaded by the repetition of similar cases. Finally, because boards can proceed without harmed parties, they may become complacent about recruiting their participation.

The models compared

Because most campuses rely on one-on-one administrative hearings to manage their caseloads, many have incorporated restorative practices into their hearings. Typically, this would include an emphasis on identifying what harm was caused by the offense and how the student can repair it. But it can also include inviting harmed parties to participate in the hearing, essentially transforming the hearing into a RJ conference.

	Conferencing	Circles	Boards
Participants	• Facilitators • Offender • Harmed parties • Support persons	• Circle keepers • Offender • Harmed parties • Support persons	• Board chair and members • Offender • Harmed parties • Support persons
Process	• Structured and unstructured dialogue	• Circle process with talking piece	• Structured and unstructured dialogue
Niche	• Featuring harmed parties • Opportunity to train pool of volunteer facilitators (students, faculty, staff)	• Including large numbers of harmed parties • Resolving mixed-responsibility conflicts • Cases with unknown offenders • Featuring campus cultural symbols and rituals	• "Victimless" and quality of life offenses • Community in general can be the harmed party • Cases when harmed parties decline participation • Easy to implement/ transition from traditional conduct board • Can include determination of responsibility
Examples	• Theft, harassment, assault, academic integrity	• Fights, roommate conflicts, bias incidents, noise	• Underage drinking, disorderly conduct, DWI, weapons possession
Tradition	• Mennonite victim-offender reconciliation programs, victim-offender mediation, and New Zealand Maori justice	• Justice practices of Native American and Canadian First Nation peoples	• Vermont Community Reparative Boards (Probation) and South African Truth and Reconciliation Commission

Deciding which practice is best for a campus depends on the goals of the initiative. Boards are often the easiest to implement because most campuses already have conduct boards in place, and they can be modified to embrace RJ principles. Conferencing can be used for a select group of RJ cases, either because the parties involved are very amenable to the process or because the incident has garnered a lot of campus attention and requires careful handling. Circle practices are especially powerful because their structured dialogue enables every person to have an equal voice in the process. They may also have a particularly spiritual quality to them and are often adopted by faith-based institutions.

Perhaps the biggest contrast between traditional conduct hearings and restorative practices is the emphasis that RJ places on identifying and repairing harm. While traditional practices focus on whether or not the student violated the conduct code, often carefully parsing which specific policy was violated, RJ dialogues explore the nature of the harm. The next chapter provides one method for this examination.

5.
Identifying Harm Using the Restorative Justice Medicine Wheel

In the popular restorative justice book, *Peacemaking Circles,* the authors note that many RJ practices and principles draw from indigenous traditions. They high-light the symbolism associated with the medicine wheel that "functions as a sacred teaching for many North and South American First Nation People."[16] Through the medicine wheel, we can discover how storytelling helps reveal the many layers of harm caused by student misconduct.

The restorative justice trainer, Duke Fisher, and I use the metaphor of the medicine wheel to highlight the importance of storytelling in the restorative justice process. The medicine wheel is composed of four quadrants. The first highlights the importance of *storytelling*—allowing each participant to describe the incident and how it affected them. The other quadrants make distinctions between *three types of harm*: material/physical, emotional/spiritual, and relational/communal.

When participants in an RJ process each have a chance to share their stories, the others see the incident from a new perspective. The facilitators take notes on how each was impacted and summarize the various harms on a flip chart.

> *"Oftentimes, it is not until we hold a circle process that students finally open up and share the truth behind their actions. The storytelling allows for the understanding in which healing immediately begins. In most circles, students come into the process with emotional walls in place. We chip away at this by having positive intake meetings, but a successful circle can break down a defensive wall and build something that is far more structurally sound."[17]*
>
> Kevin D. Mowers
> Assistant Director of Student Conduct and
> Conflict Resolution, Residence Education
> University of Michigan

At the University of Michigan, a first year student—we'll call her "Rachel"—returned to her residence hall highly intoxicated late on a Thursday night.[18] A friend of hers confronted her for being so drunk, and the two got into a loud argument. A housing security officer determined that Rachel needed to be hospitalized, and Rachel became belligerent, ripping down door decorations, screaming, swearing at and then hitting the officer, and resisting the ambulance staff. Eventually, she was transported to the emergency room and treated for her intoxication.

Later, Rachel was embarrassed by what had happened and expressed remorse but still did not understand the wider implications of her behavior. Two trained undergraduate facilitators convened a restorative justice circle. In addition to Rachel, twelve impacted parties attended, including the hall director, resident advisor, housing security officer, and hall residents.

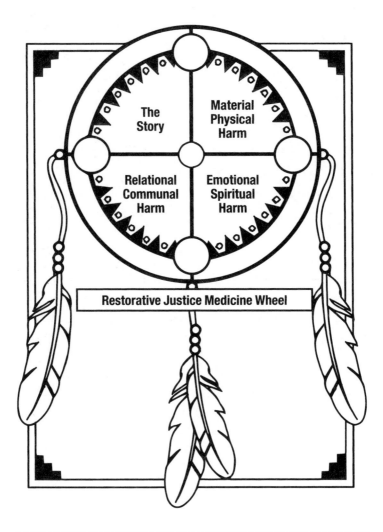

Restorative Justice Medicine Wheel

During the storytelling process, Rachel was able to hear about how she had impacted others in the community. She was also able to share what it was like to be transported to the hospital, receive an underage drinking citation, and face her roommate and the hall community after the incident. She shared her desire to repair her reputation with the community and to not be defined by this incident.

This unfortunately-common offense illustrates the three varieties of harm in the medicine wheel. Rachel caused *material/physical harm* when she assaulted the housing security officer and when she tore down the door decorations. She caused *emotional/spiritual harm* when she became belligerent and confrontational towards her friend, the officer, and the ambulance staff. She caused *relational/communal harm* when she woke up other residents, causing a variety of responses including fear for their own safety, worry that someone was being hurt, and anger at being awakened when they had classes to attend first thing in the morning. The participants were also able to share their concerns about Rachel's trustworthiness given her drinking behavior, as well as the more general problem of binge drinking on campus.

Agreements seek to address the needs of harmed parties.

By carefully listing the various harms, the circle was able to form an agreement that addressed their needs. Rachel provided a verbal apology during the circle and agreed to do something for each of the individuals impacted. For some, she made new door decorations, and for others, she attended an event or had a meal with them. She baked cookies for the housing security officer and wrote a personal note acknowledging the importance of the officer's work. She also planned and coordinated an alternative-to-alcohol event later that semester and attended an alcohol education program that taught her harm reduction strategies.

Many conduct administrators believe that consistency is important: similar violations should lead to similar sanctions. In restorative justice, sanctions are tailored to the needs and concerns of the circle participants as they are identified in the storytelling process. This approach recognizes the complexities of each incident. Two alcohol transports may be identical in how they are listed as conduct violations but quite different in the harms caused, the attitude and risk level

RJ recognizes the complexity of each incident.

of the offender, and the will of the group for the best response to the situation.

The process of identifying harm is important because it helps the offender to understand the consequences of his or her behavior and allows the participants to specifically address them in the agreement. The next chapter provides suggestions about how to make RJ sanctions as successful as possible.

6.
Best Practices in Repairing Harm and Rebuilding Trust

Rupert Ross, a Canadian attorney and prosecutor, has written about his experience using restorative justice with First Nations communities. He observed, "An offender cannot even *know* what he did until he begins to learn, first-hand and in a feeling way, how people were affected by it."[19]

The first question we ask in a restorative process acknowledges that harm has taken place. A restorative dialogue includes an exploration about the nature of this harm. This is why it is so important to include people who were impacted by the offense. By including harmed parties, offenders have a chance to learn about the actual harm caused by their behavior.

Once the harm is identified, the participants can explore how the harm can be repaired. Solutions often include a combination of tasks that respond to three kinds of harm: emotional/spiritual harm, material/physical harm, and relational/communal harm. Apologies are a response to emotional harm. Restitution addresses material harm. Community service mends the social fabric.

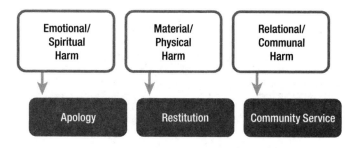

Apology guidelines

"An apology is a good way to have the last word."
Author unknown

Apologies are expressions of remorse and the willingness to take responsibility for a transgression. They must be sincere if they are to be taken seriously. Apologies are an important way to repair community relationships and restore trust between parties. When apologies are assigned as a sanction, they should be written (not verbal) and approved before sending to a harmed party.

Apology letters should include:

What happened
- A description detailing the harm caused by the offense. This shows that the offender understands the harmful consequences of his or her behavior.

My role
  • An acknowledgement that the offender was responsible for the offense. Watch out for expressions that deny, displace, or minimize responsibility.

How I feel
  • An expression of remorse or regret in causing harm.

What I won't do
  • A statement of commitment to responsible behavior and causing no further trouble.

What I will do
  • A statement of commitment to make amends for the harm caused.

Student offenders often spontaneously provide verbal apologies during RJ conferences, and these are important moments in the dialogue. It is not expected that they will capture all of the elements of the written apology guidelines. The same is true for first drafts. Mentoring a student through the apology-writing process is a tremendous student development opportunity.

Restitution guidelines

Restitution is monetary payment or labor that pays for financial losses. Labor can be defined broadly to include creative projects or symbolic activities such as an art student who pays restitution to the harmed party by painting her portrait. Restitution is very different from fines even though they can both involve money. Fines are a punitive sanction meant to impose a cost or burden upon the offender and usually go to the institution. The amount is determined by what is believed to be effective in deterring repeat offending. Restitution is determined by an accounting of the losses incurred by the harmed party and goes to the harmed party.

Restitution agreements should include:

Monetary losses
- Clear specification of financial or property losses to the harmed party.

Payment plan
- A payment plan that meets the needs of the harmed party, but also takes into account the offender's ability to pay.
- Sometimes labor or other creative endeavors are substituted for payment.

Community service guidelines

Volunteering in the community is a way to be helpful to others, show that one is socially responsible, and rebuild the trust that is lost through misbehavior. Community service should be meaningful and rewarding. It can be an excellent opportunity for the offender to learn new skills, practically examine a personal value, and develop new relationships with positive peers and mentors. Community service can fulfill two important goals:

- Service is a way of making amends to the community.
- Service is an opportunity to demonstrate good citizenship.

Community service projects should include:

Proposal

- Offenders should take the lead on proposing a relevant form of community service. Proposals should include:
  - The type of service project.
  - How the service makes amends for harm done to the community.
  - Learning goals for the offender's personal development.
  - A timeline for service completion.

Validation

- A letter, signed by a service agency staff member, to verify that the project was completed satisfactorily.

Reflection

- A letter describing the value of service experience personally and for the community.

Consider, for example, two Skidmore College roommates who took lounge furniture into their room while also leaving the common area a mess. A turning point in their RJ conference happened when another student, who worked as a tour guide, described how embarrassing it was to show the residence hall to prospective students in the condition they had left it. In response, the roommates recognized an important harm and proposed organizing a dorm-wide "spring cleaning" in preparation for a major admissions event. This kind of community service helped repair the harm they had caused while also providing the offenders a way to be positive leaders on campus.

Trust-building activities

In addition to repairing harm, when a student commits a violation, it is natural and appropriate for the campus community to question his or her trustworthiness. A restorative dialogue helps the participants come to understand why the offender chose to engage in the misbehavior. It helps to identify positive actions that he or she could undertake that will help reassure everyone that the behavior will not be repeated. An RJ dialogue is focused on how the student can demonstrate responsibility and learn to be a trustworthy member of the campus community.

Suspension may be an outcome when the RJ process cannot identify a viable strategy for reintegration. RJ participants are concerned with the question, "What will reassure us that you

> **Suspension may be an outcome when RJ cannot identify a viable alternative for reintegration.**

will be a positive member of the campus community?" Often, such reassurance occurs when the offender commits to involvements that reduce the likelihood that they will reoffend. These involvements can include: seeking counseling; activities that show how they can be positive members of the community like running for a leadership position; and/or activities that help them further explore and understand the harm they caused such as a research project about the issue and organizing a campus program to educate other students about it.

An example of trust building

A highly-intoxicated University of Florida student confronted his ex-girlfriend about their break-up. As they argued, he got into her car and refused to leave. So she drove to the campus police station where he had to be physically removed by several officers. A restorative justice conference was convened, and the participants debated whether or not he should be able to return to the institution. Although it helped that he was very remorseful and had no prior disciplinary record, the participants, particularly four law enforcement officers, really needed to be persuaded. To do this, the student agreed that he would seek counseling to address anger, relationship, and substance abuse issues. In addition, he agreed to collaborate with the police officers to present a campus workshop on the legal ramifications of alcohol and drug use.

> *"Law enforcement often refers cases to student conduct and then never hears an outcome or doesn't understand why a student is still on campus or has returned to campus. In this case, RJ allowed for law enforcement to have a say in the outcome and provided them with a better understanding of the student besides what they saw at the time of the incident."*[20]
>
> Chris Loschiavo
> Director of Student Conduct and Conflict Resolution
> University of Florida

RJ does not rely simply on an offender's promise to be good; in this case, it was his active role in seeking counseling and a service project that strengthened his ties to campus police while showing a positive leadership role that rebuilt community trust.

Just as it is important for an offender to demonstrate his or her reliability, it is important to determine if RJ is as effective in meeting its goals. The next chapter reviews recent research on the use of RJ in campus conduct.

7.
Does it Work?
Research and Assessment
of Campus Restorative
Programs

To explore the effectiveness of campus restorative justice, I recently conducted a study called the STARR Project (STudent Accountability and Restorative Research Project).[21] The research team gathered data on 659 conduct cases from eighteen schools throughout the United States, including large public institutions and liberal arts colleges, both secular and faith-based. We compared restorative practices with traditional model code hearings.

Appeals, completion, and reoffending

RJ and model code hearings tend to produce similarly low numbers of appeals, high rates of program completion, and relatively few repeat offenders. Appeals were rare overall, but practically nonexistent in RJ cases (less than one percent). This was less than in model code cases, which had an appeal rate of four percent. Both practices had similarly high rates of compliance, with ninety-three percent of students completing their sanctions within one year of the hearing. And both practices had similar rates of reoffending, about eighteen percent within one year. However, when students reoffended after an RJ intervention, their violations tended to be less serious than model code reoffenders.

Participant satisfaction

In the STARR Project, RJ practices sharply contrasted with model code hearings by their inclusion of harmed parties in the dialogue process. The table below shows that harmed parties consistently and strongly appreciated this opportunity for participation.[22]

Harmed Party Satisfaction With Restorative Justice Process

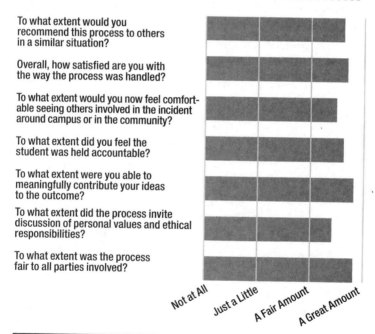

To what extent would you recommend this process to others in a similar situation?

Overall, how satisfied are you with the way the process was handled?

To what extent would you now feel comfortable seeing others involved in the incident around campus or in the community?

To what extent did you feel the student was held accountable?

To what extent were you able to meaningfully contribute your ideas to the outcome?

To what extent did the process invite discussion of personal values and ethical responsibilities?

To what extent was the process fair to all parties involved?

Not at All · Just a Little · A Fair Amount · A Great Amount

Student learning

Student affairs professionals are *educators* and recognize that when students get in trouble, there is opportunity to use the conduct process to teach them important life lessons about the responsibilities of community membership. In the STARR Project, we explored six dimensions of student learning and found that restorative practices created an excellent opportunity for learning.[23] In each case, RJ yielded statistically significant improvements in learning over model code hearings.

Student Offender Learning Outcomes

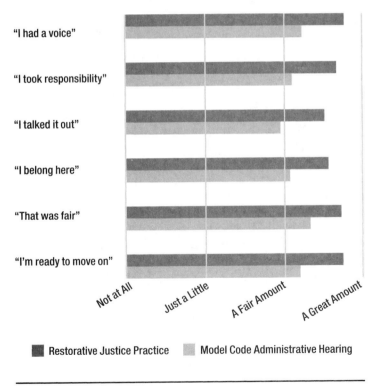

■ Restorative Justice Practice   ▨ Model Code Administrative Hearing

The categories

"I had a voice" refers to the active participation of the offender in the decision-making process. It has the student development goal of internalizing community standards so behavior is guided by conscience and recognition of the ethical responsibilities inherent in community membership.

"I took responsibility" refers to how much offenders understand not only that the behavior was a violation of rules, but also the consequences of the behavior for others, and to their willingness to take responsibility for making things right.

"I talked it out" refers to the ability to listen to others' perspectives, express remorse, and repair fractured relationships at least to the point that students in conflict can safely and civilly co-exist in the campus community.

"I belong here" refers to the student's social ties to the campus community, including a positive, non-adversarial orientation to campus administrators and police.

"That was fair" refers to the belief that the conduct process was fair, which helps create a sense of legitimacy for the rules and standards of the institution.

"I'm ready to move on" refers to satisfaction with the process leading to closure: facing up to the misconduct, learning from it, but not letting it become an obstacle to future success.

Overall, these findings are very encouraging. They suggest that it is possible to effectively respond to the needs of harmed parties while holding student offenders accountable in a way that enhances student learning and development. Participants believe the process is fair and this was a meaningful way to hold the offenders accountable for their misbehavior.

8.
Restorative Justice and Social Justice

College campuses are using restorative practices to respond to bias incidents as an approach to improving campus climate. For example, the University of California Office of the President has recommended that each of its ten campuses explore the use of RJ "when dealing with incidents of intolerance or hate, particularly for conduct that, while offensive, may not violate any laws or policies."[24]

At Colorado State University (CSU), two floormates in a residence hall got along poorly, and one of them called the other a "chink." Later, in the dining hall, the harmed party, who was Asian, responded by loudly yelling, "This is the reason that stuff like Virginia Tech happens!"—referring to the 2007 incident when a student, Seung-Hui Cho, shot and killed thirty-two people and wounded seventeen others. CSU's restorative justice program held a restorative conference that included, among others, the student offender, his coach who served as his support person, the harmed party, and his support person.

The conference enabled the participants to speak openly about several important issues and come up with a restorative agreement that best addressed their concerns. The harmed party was able to communicate that the name-calling was offensive to him and caused him to feel marginalized during an already difficult transition to college. The offender acknowledged this, apologized, and shared his own challenges in making the transition. His coach helped the offender realize that some students have built-in support networks, such as a team, while others face more of a challenge finding their place in a large and often impersonal university. The harmed party was able to share that his outburst about Virginia Tech was not meant to be a threat and was able to reassure the participants that he did not intend to hurt anyone.

The conference created an agreement with several elements. The offender agreed not only to behave positively

> *"I just don't think there is an educational workshop or other sanction that can duplicate sitting in front of the person you harmed and hearing how it affected them. I believe it is actually much more difficult to do this than simply showing up to a workshop."*[25]
>
> Paul Osincup
> Associate Director of Conflict Resolution and
> Conduct Services, Colorado State University

toward the harmed party, but that he would do what he could to ensure no one else on their floor would feel bullied for the rest of their year together. The coach offered to take the harmed party to watch a practice or game as a strategy to help him feel less isolated and to build a positive relationship with the athlete/offender. The harmed party formed a plan to meet with the director of the Asian/Pacific American Cultural Center, also as a strategy for him to find community at CSU.

Restorative justice is used as a strategy for community building and improving campus climate. Cases like this one help remind us that participants in any restorative process come from different backgrounds with varying degrees of social power. As a facilitator, it is vital to pay attention to social inequalities and try to offset power imbalances. RJ facilitators are not neutral or impartial, descriptions that might imply that we are indifferent, objective, disengaged, unemotional, or value-free. Instead, we are "multipartial," actively supporting all participants without preference or taking sides.

Typical power imbalances

- ≠ Offenders/harmed parties (sometimes harmed parties are afraid to speak to offenders)
- ≠ Harmed parties/offenders (sometimes offenders are overcome by shame)
- ≠ Facilitators/participants (facilitators can subconsciously steer the dialogue)
- ≠ Faculty/staff/students (students may be deferential to faculty or staff)
- ≠ Key stakeholders/less affected participants (less affected parties may not believe their needs are as important as those of others)
- ≠ Social identities (race, class, gender, sexuality, ability, religion)
- ≠ Group size (ratio of participants on offender's side/victim's side can affect how well participants feel supported)

Three of the more explicit expressions of power are (1) coalition-building—persuading other participants to accept one point of view, (2) air time—dominating the discussion, interrupting, not listening, and (3) inflexibility—stubborn refusal to move from stated position.

Multipartial facilitation techniques

- = Keep social power in your awareness: Assess the group and anticipate expressions of power.
- = Co-facilitate with someone of a different social identity.
- = Balance airtime: Invite quiet members to share; use the circle process with a talking piece.
- = First person narratives: Invite "I statements" and personal sharing; discourage judgmental claims and attributions.
- = Create space for quiet reflection: Enable participants to gather their thoughts before speaking.
- = Be encouraging: Notice body language and facial expressions of raw emotion such as shame, sadness, or hopelessness, and help participants see the opportunity the dialogue is providing to help meet needs and find resolution.
- = Model authenticity and vulnerability: Share relevant stories (but do not shift the focus from participants to the facilitator).
- = Bring power dynamics to the surface: Identify out loud what you are observing. Ask for clarification. Take the lead. Don't rely on less powerful individuals to challenge oppressive statements.

9.
Starting a Program

Launching a new program can be a daunting process, especially in times of shrinking campus resources. Most conduct officers complain that they are overburdened with cases, backlogged with email messages, and can never predict which day will bring a new student crisis. Building any new program is certainly time-consuming, and many would argue that RJ cases are more time-consuming than traditional administrative hearings. But it is also possible to refocus staff energy from hearing cases to training and managing RJ volunteers, a new and very empowering role that might increase morale and staff retention.

In addition to offering a few questions below that help bring focus to the implementation process, I have asked for insights about implementation from two esteemed colleagues who have recently introduced restorative justice to their campuses.

Questions About Implementation

- What kind of restorative justice process resonates best with your campus culture or with the kinds of cases on which your program will focus? Conferencing, circles, boards?

- In what ways can you infuse RJ principles into current conduct practices and procedures?
- What opportunities or constraints currently exist in your code of conduct for implementing an RJ program?
- Where do you need to foster support for the program? Student affairs administrators, legal counsel, campus safety, student government?
- Where will the program be housed? Conduct office, residential life, conflict resolution program?
- Do you have the right staff for a restorative justice program? Who will coordinate the program? Could the coordinating responsibilities be added to a current position?
- Who will facilitate cases—staff, faculty, graduate students, undergraduates?
- How much will a program cost? What costs do you need to consider? Do you have financial support? How will you pay for the program?
- Can you connect/collaborate with a local restorative justice program? Are there possible partnerships with faculty or academic departments (higher education management, law, criminal justice, conflict analysis, peace studies, social work, etc.)? What other resources can you utilize?
- How will you launch and market the program?
- What will be your referral streams? How can referrals be promoted?
- How would you implement training for the program? Who needs to receive training?

- How will you assess the effectiveness of your RJ program?

◇◇◇◇◇◇◇◇◇◇◇◇◇◇◇◇◇◇◇◇◇◇◇◇◇◇◇◇◇◇◇◇◇◇◇

Sonoo Thadaney Israni
Restorative Justice Pilot Program Manager
Stanford University

Many campuses, keen to explore restorative justice programs, frequently ask facilitators of Stanford's RJ pilot, "How did you get started?" Our Vice Provost of Student Affairs and Associate Vice Provost/ Dean of Student Life have been interested in exploring alternative dispute resolutions to address student conduct issues. Peer mediation and restorative justice were priorities. Fortunately, we have also had support from alumni who are practitioners in the field and have supported us with their wisdom and funding.

Steps that launched Stanford's RJ pilot

1. Received leadership support from our Associate Vice Provost/Dean of Student Life and John Krumboltz, Professor of Education and Psychology, who teaches a course, cross-listed in both Education and Psychology, entitled Mediation for Dispute Resolution.
2. Received funding and support from alumni, donors, and foundation.
3. Hired experienced RJ practitioner as program manager (twenty-five percent FTE).
4. Researched existing RJ programs and shared with campus partners and leadership for feedback and customization.

5. Program manager attended two-day campus RJ training at Skidmore College.
6. Developed program manual ensuring its alignment with existing mandates, protocols, and processes.
7. Customized assessment forms for respondents, harmed parties, facilitators, and observers.
8. Recruited volunteer facilitators including students and colleagues with experience in RJ and mediation and provided program orientation and facilitator training.
9. Scheduled a standard bi-weekly meeting time for case facilitation, case debriefing, and ongoing training. We found evenings to be most convenient and offered simple meals to build community and show appreciation.

◇◇◇◇◇◇◇◇◇◇◇◇◇◇◇◇◇◇◇◇◇◇◇◇◇◇◇◇◇◇◇

Deborah Eerkes
Director, Office of Student Judicial Affairs
University of Alberta

Prior to implementing our RJ program, the University of Alberta Residence Community Standards formed a cumbersome document, containing variations on the student conduct theme for each of the different residence halls. Eventually, the policy became too unwieldy to maintain, and the committee with primary oversight for student conduct policies demanded change.

Using all of the existing structures but replacing the underlying punitive principles with restorative ones, a new policy was drafted. Existing positions were retooled (for example, a student conduct administrator became a restorative agreement administrator), and conduct hearings were converted to restorative team meetings.

What followed was a marathon of consultation meetings sponsored by the Dean of Students with various campus stakeholders. Shifting the mindset from punitive to restorative proved challenging, and it became clear that reassurances were necessary. As part of the transition plan, we engaged local and international experts to assist in the training and roll-out of the program and committed to reviewing the program after each of the first and second years. With those assurances in place, the Board of Governors approved the new Residence Community Standards.

Residence Life and Judicial Affairs staff spent the summer designing training sessions, compiling manuals and other resources, and promoting the new program among staff and students. New staff was recruited using the updated job descriptions, and after training by both local and external RJ practitioners, the program went into effect.

Top five lessons learned at the University of Alberta
1. It was critical to have the support of the Provost and the Dean of Students before bringing an RJ program forward to the community for approval.
2. It was easier to adapt RJ to fit into our culture than to change our culture to accommodate RJ. The beauty of RJ is that it adapts to any environment and by its very nature changes a culture over time.
3. We needed to carefully answer the policy and program questions outlined in the beginning of this chapter during the first stage of our implementation.

4. It was impossible to pay too much attention to staff training and promotion of the program. Staff understanding and buy-in of the program was the key to our success. They are the ambassadors of the program and mentor students in its use and application. Training needed to be intensive and ongoing; promotion needed to be extensive and engaging.

5. We were flexible enough to adapt the processes when they were not working as envisioned. We continued to embrace the basic principles of identifying and repairing harm and rebuilding trust but allowed for those things to happen in the most appropriate ways.

◇◇◇◇◇◇◇◇◇◇◇◇◇◇◇◇◇◇◇◇◇◇◇◇◇◇◇◇◇◇◇

Challenges to implementation

Starting an RJ program poses some dilemmas for campuses. One is the problem of case referrals. Most campuses are cautious about this new approach and wish to refer only the most minor cases. But those often have the least tangible harm, such as underage alcohol possession or marijuana possession.

RJ cases are most effective in cases that have clearly identifiable harms, which help the participants shift from the mindset of punishing code violations to repairing harm and rebuilding trust. So implementing a new program requires a small leap of faith in its first case referrals to ensure that more serious cases are included.

A similar leap of faith is required with facilitation and training. It is best to use experienced facilitators, but a new program will not have these. It is also best to use trainers that have facilitation and implementation experience, but again, a new program may not have such staff readily available. Partnerships with community-based RJ programs is one solution, working with training consultants is another, but campuses must work quickly and deliberately to develop internal capacity and expertise. The next chapter offers tips on how to offer an RJ training.

10.
Facilitating a Restorative Justice Training

A campus RJ training should help participants gain a thorough understanding of restorative justice principles and practices, strong facilitation skills, practical information about program implementation, and the satisfaction of having participated in an intellectually and emotionally rewarding training experience.

Because RJ elicits both moral dialogue and raw emotions, it is important to create an experiential training environment that feels realistic to participants. Most are not really sold on the idea of RJ until they have experienced it in role play or observed an actual case. While there is much information to be shared, it is best done through dialogue and active learning rather than through lecture or PowerPoint presentation.

Designing the training

How much training is necessary? This will vary according to four key constituencies, each requiring increasing levels of training.

RJ advocates are individuals who do not participate in the program but need to know enough about it to

---

advocate for it. They might be a dean or professor or student leader. A few hours of training are probably sufficient for this group.

RJ facilitators must have a thorough understanding of RJ principles and facilitation skills in at least one method of practice (such as conferencing).

RJ program coordinators should be able to mentor facilitators as well as understand the nuts and bolts of program implementation from revising conduct codes to case management.

RJ trainers should have on-the-ground experience with case facilitation as well as a broad understanding of types of practices and the global landscape of restorative justice.

Below is list of training topics and intended audiences. Each module is approximately three hours.

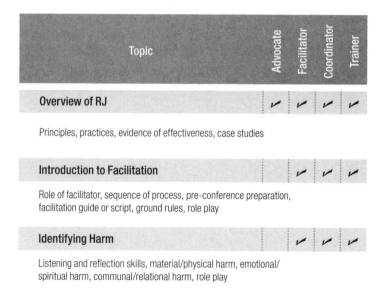

Topic	Advocate	Facilitator	Coordinator	Trainer
Overview of RJ	✔	✔	✔	✔
Principles, practices, evidence of effectiveness, case studies				
Introduction to Facilitation		✔	✔	✔
Role of facilitator, sequence of process, pre-conference preparation, facilitation guide or script, ground rules, role play				
Identifying Harm		✔	✔	✔
Listening and reflection skills, material/physical harm, emotional/spiritual harm, communal/relational harm, role play				

Topic	Advocate	Facilitator	Coordinator	Trainer
RJ Outcomes	✔	✔	✔	
Identifying harm, apologies, restitution, community service, rebuilding trust				
Issues in Facilitation	✔	✔	✔	
Diversity and inclusion, secondary victimization, denial of responsibility, character judgments, role play				
Implementation		✔	✔	
Program models, referrals, case management, marketing a program, training, policy updates				
Train-the-trainer				✔
Active learning, lesson planning, practice and coaching				

Many organizations provide training in restorative practices. Ideally, resources can be found locally by contacting community-based programs or faculty on campus. Some training resources, such as film clips and role plays, are posted on my website: www.CampusRJ.com. The Association for Student Conduct Administration may offer referrals as would the International Institute for Restorative Practices.

11.
Preparing for a
Restorative Justice
Conference

Most practitioners emphasize the importance of preparing people for participation in an RJ conference. Unlike mediation practice, where facilitators frequently know little about the dispute, RJ facilitators gather as much information as they can beforehand. This is necessary because the risk of revictimization is reduced when facilitators know the perspectives of the participants and what they are likely to say during the conference.

The RJ facilitator makes contact with all participants before the RJ conference in order to assess the appropriateness of holding the conference. The facilitator discusses the process of the conference and its potential value for the participants. The pre-conference process is an opportunity to build trust with the facilitator and have all questions answered.

Pre-Conference Meeting With Person Responsible (Offender)

Re-introduce yourself:
- Your role and connection to this conference.

Describe the conferencing process simply and clearly:
- Review the basic steps and the questions that will be asked.
- Summarize the collaborative decision-making process to identify and repair the harm and to rebuild trust.

Present benefits of conferencing:
- Have direct input in the outcome of the process.
- Opportunity to explain what happened from your perspective.
- Chance to express remorse and take responsibility.
- Ability to share who you are beyond this one mistake.
- Learn about everyone's perspectives and concerns.
- Include support person of your choice.
- Tried and true process.

Hear the story:
- Paraphrase/reflect feelings.
- Allow for silence.
- Listen for acceptance/denial of responsibility.
- Listen for ability to express affect/emotion.
- Listen for red flags that would make case inappropriate for conferencing.

Describe the conferencing process in more detail:
- Who will be there.
- Voluntary process.
- Facilitators are multipartial and trained.
- Confidential (applies only to facilitators), except if imminent danger.
- Focus on repairing harm and rebuilding trust, not on punishment or passing judgment.
- Agreement, if signed, is binding.
- Agreements might include apology letters, restitution, community service, etc.

Ask for ideas about how to repair harm and rebuild trust.
Address any concerns the offender may have.
Discuss whether or not offender wants to participate.
Identify potential support person.
Get and provide contact information.
Schedule tentative date, time, and location.

Pre-Conference Meeting With Harmed Party

Re-introduce yourself:
- Your role and connection to this conference.

Describe the conferencing process simply and clearly:
- Review the basic steps and the questions that will be asked.
- Summarize the collaborative decision-making process to identify and repair the harm and to rebuild trust.

Present benefits of conferencing:
- Opportunity to meet with person responsible in a safe environment, which is often helpful for harmed parties.
- Chance to express how you were/are affected.
- Receive information about the misconduct directly from person responsible.
- Have direct input in outcome of misconduct.
- Include support person of your choice.
- Tried and true process.

Hear the story:
- Paraphrase/reflect feelings.
- Acknowledge harm.
- Allow for silence.
- Listen for red flags that would make case inappropriate for conferencing.

Describe the conferencing process in more detail:
- Who will be there.
- Voluntary process.
- Facilitators are multipartial and trained.
- Confidential (applies only to facilitators), except if imminent danger.
- Focus on repairing harm and rebuilding trust, not on punishment or passing judgment.
- Agreement, if signed, is binding.
- Agreements might include apology letters, restitution, community service, etc.

Ask what they would like to see happen to address the harm:
- Listen for needs that could potentially be met or not met by the conferencing process.

Address any concerns the harmed party may have.
Discuss whether or not the harmed party wants to participate.
Identify potential support person.
Get and provide contact information.
Schedule tentative date, time, and location.

Red flags

It is the facilitators' job to decide if the case is appropriate for an RJ conference. The following is a short list of considerations. Of course, flags are never fully red—there are always grey areas that require thoughtful judgment.

Voluntary process: The conference should not go forward if the offender or harmed parties feel coerced into participation. While this may seem easy to assess, many programs offer incentives such as not having the offense appear on the student's disciplinary record. Incentives are fine, but facilitators must assess whether or not participants feel unduly pressured.

Admission of responsibility: With the exception of RJ boards, restorative practices minimally expect that the offender has admitted the misconduct. Even so, it is common for offenders to dispute some of the facts of the case, to deflect responsibility ("I did it, but it was my roommate's idea, not mine") or minimize the harm ("Everyone does this; it's no big deal").

Some programs refer cases to RJ only when the offender expresses deep remorse; others use the RJ process to help offenders understand the harm and learn to take full responsibility.

Victim safety: The goal of RJ is to help harmed parties, not cause further damage. Facilitators must keep this in mind during pre-conference meetings. Will the offender engage in victim-blaming? How fragile does the victim appear?

Mental health: Facilitators are not in a position to make clinical diagnoses, and RJ conferences are not designed as therapeutic interventions. Clear signs of mental illness are an indication that the participant may not be able to listen effectively or be capable of representing him or herself.

12.
Conference Facilitator Apprentice Script

Many RJ practitioners debate the value of using an RJ script. Some believe it is important to follow one closely to ensure consistent practice. For example, if one harmed party is asked a specific question like, "What do you think needs to happen to make things right?" then it is important to ask another harmed party the same question. Other practitioners, however, like to rely on well-developed group facilitation skills that enable them to be responsive to the situation and guide the conversation in unplanned directions.

My solution to this is to provide an "apprentice script,"[26] which can be followed closely for those who want to rely on a clear set of prompts, but also (in the left column) highlights topics to be addressed to help practitioners maintain a coherent flow without binding them to particular questions.

In general, the flow of dialogue is illustrated as follows. The pattern begins with the offender or "person responsible," who describes the incident first. Often harmed parties are reticent to speak until they have heard from the offender first. In this script, the offender speaks first, but some facilitators will invite the

---

participants to decide who will speak first. After the harmed parties speak, the flow returns to the offender again so that he or she can respond to what others have said.

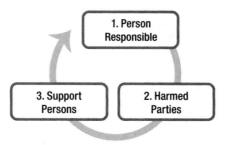

The next illustration is a guide to seating arrangements. Offenders are placed close to a facilitator and their support person. Harmed parties and offenders are ideally situated on opposite sides of the circle so that they have some distance between them, but can also look at and speak directly to each other. The seating template also highlights a common division of labor between facilitators. One tends to open the conference, hosting the conversation while the other takes notes. However, as the dialogue shifts to the listing of harms and brainstorming solutions, the second facilitator usually takes over.

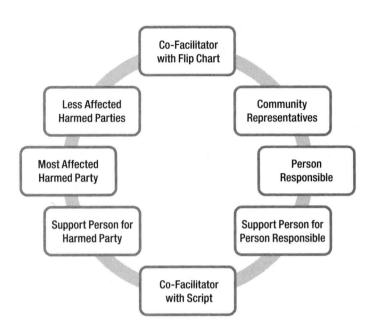

What to do right before the conference:

- Ensure that your facilitation instruments are all ready (script, seating plan, flip chart and markers, pen/pads, incident summary, name tags).
- Before the participants arrive, arrange the seating according to your seating plan.
- Be ready to greet the participants upon arrival, and invite harmed parties and person responsible (offender) to wait in separate areas.
- When everyone is ready, invite the participants into the conference room, and show them to their seats. Seat any observers and secondary stakeholders first, harmed parties next, and the person responsible last, especially if the conference is large.

Introduction

Bulleted Script	Example Text
• Welcome	**To everybody:** Welcome everybody. Before the formal part of the conference begins, please silence your cell phones. The conference will last approximately two hours. I would like us to introduce ourselves and indicate briefly our reasons for being here. I am [co-facilitatator's name], and I will be co-facilitating today's conference. Let's go around the circle. Please tell us your name and your connection to this conference today.
• Round of introductions (name/role)	Thank you for attending. At today's conference, we will be focusing on the [incident] that happened on [date]. We will focus on what [*first name of person responsible*] did and its impact on others. Once we have learned more about what happened, we will identify what harm was caused and how it might be repaired. We will also focus on what can be done to reassure us that the behavior will not be repeated.
• Agreement to be approved by associate dean	This conference is voluntary. We do not have to reach an agreement today, and if we do not, the case will be referred back to the Associate Dean of Student Affairs and handled in a different way. I am hopeful that we will reach an agreement and if so, we will submit it to the dean for approval. It is possible, but rare, that the dean will want to make changes to the agreement. Does everybody understand this?
• Ground rules	One goal of this conference is to create an environment in which everyone can speak freely and fully about how they feel about what happened. As facilitators, our job is to ensure that everyone here has a voice. Sometimes we will have open dialogue in which everyone can participate as they wish; at other times we will go around the circle inviting each person to offer their perspective. When we do, a person can always pass if they do not have anything they want to say at that time. Another job for us as facilitators is to create an environment of trust, so that we can speak honestly about the incident. To enable this, will everyone agree that what is said in this circle will stay in the circle—that we will not talk about what people have said here to others?

• Academic and co-curricular involvement of person responsible	*To person responsible:* We would like to begin by getting to know you. What classes are you taking this semester? What is your major? How are you involved on campus? Clubs? Activities? What do you hope will come of this discussion today?

Harm Identification

Bulleted Script	Example Text
	Co-facilitator takes notes. When everyone has spoken, the notes are summarized, and harms are listed on a flipchart. Then the group is asked for confirmation and completeness. All questions below are suggested prompts. Facilitator can modify as appropriate. *To everybody:* Now we will learn about the incident by asking everyone to tell us about what happened from their perspective. We will start with the person(s) responsible, then hear from harmed parties, and then support persons. Let's start with [*person responsible*] because that is where this all began.
• Person responsible	*To person responsible:* What happened? What were you thinking of at the time? What have you thought about since? Who has been affected by what you have done? In what way? What do you think you need to do to make things right? Is there anything else you would like to say or ask at this time? *Repeat for additional responsible parties, if any.*
• Harmed parties	*To harmed parties:* What happened from your perspective? What impact has this incident had on you? What has been the hardest thing for you? What do you think needs to happen to make things right? Is there anything else you would like to say or ask at this time?

• Support persons	**To support persons:** Is there anything you would like to say or ask at this point?
• Person responsible	**To person responsible:** You have now had a chance to hear about how the incident has affected everyone. Is there anything you would like to say at this time?

Listing Harms

• Communicate that you were taking notes, want to check for accuracy	*Facilitators may wish to shift primary leadership at this point and have the facilitator who has been listing harms lead the review of them and the brainstorming process to find solutions.* **To everybody:** We will now summarize our list of harms.
• List harms on flip chart	Is there anything to be changed or added?
• Check for accuracy	*Check in with participants beginning with harmed parties to confirm that you have correctly identified and listed harms. Use clear, brief, specific language while flip charting. Don't "smooth over" language, e.g., list "broken window," not "window," and "fear walking outside at night," not "safe campus."*

Agreement Process

Bulleted Script	Example Text
• Have list of harms	*Start a new flip chart page called "solutions."*
• Explore how to make things right	**To everybody:** We have all spoken about the harms caused by this incident and are now at the stage of identifying what can be done to make things right. Two basic questions will guide us forward: 1. How can the harm be repaired? 2. How can we regain confidence in [*person responsible*] so that we can trust that s/he will be a responsible member of our community?

• How can harm be repaired? • How can we rebuild trust?	Please remember that our focus is on finding solutions. We are not here to decide if [*person responsible*] is a good or bad person, but to figure out how the harm can be repaired and trust rebuilt.
• Check for agreement to proceed	If you do not believe we can work on solutions together, we can discuss this and, perhaps, end the conference. Would you like to continue with the conference?
• Break, if desired	*If no, then end conference, explaining that the case will be referred back to the associate dean and handled in another way. Thank participants for their willingness to bring the details of the harm to light. Dismiss participants.* *If yes, state the conference is about halfway done. Ask participants if they would like to take a short break before continuing.* *If you go on a break, it is okay if participants talk informally, but pay attention to the tone, and keep the break short.*

Brainstorming Solutions

	This next stage is about coming up with ideas. We will write all of the suggestions on the flipchart. Later we can decide to make changes and finalize an agreement that is satisfactory to everyone. During this brainstorming process, we will post all of your ideas on the flipchart. Later, we can refine them and write up the agreement.
• Ask person responsible how the harm could be repaired • Ask person responsible how trust can be restored	**To person responsible:** Looking at this list of harms, what do you think can be done to repair them? What else can you do to demonstrate that you can be a positive member of our community?

• Check with harmed parties for their ideas to repair the harm and regain trust	**To harmed parties sequentially, then support persons:** Looking at this list of harms, what do you think can be done to repair them? What else would you need to see from [*person responsible*] to restore your confidence in him/her?
• Check for collective agreement	**To everybody:** What do you think of what we have come up with so far? Let's make sure we have a plan that best addresses our concerns and is also fair and reasonable.
• Check back with person responsible	**To person responsible:** Would you be able to agree to these suggestions? Do you have any concerns that we should address?

Finalizing Agreement

• Communicate that the agreement will be submitted to the associate dean for approval	**To everybody:** Now that we have reached an agreement, we will submit it to the associate dean for approval.
• Communicate consequences for not fulfilling terms of the agreement (i.e., hold on housing and class registration)	**To everybody:** If the agreement is accepted by the associate dean, then [*person responsible*] will have to complete the various tasks by the deadline or he/she will not be able to register for next semester's classes (or will have his/her diploma held if a graduating senior).

• Appeals process	**To person responsible:** If after you leave, you believe that this process was conducted unfairly, you can appeal the agreement we have reached with the associate dean.
• Evaluation forms	**To everybody:** While we write up the agreement, we would like you to complete an evaluation form. This will help us to know how well this process worked for you and how we can improve it. *Pass out and collect forms. Have agreement signed and pass out copies.*

Closing

Bulleted Script	Example Text
	Try to end on a positive note by expressing appreciation for the hard work completed
• Thank you	**To everybody:** Thank you for your hard work today.
• Final round— how are you feeling about how things went?	In closing this conference, I'd like to go around the circle and ask each person how he or she is feeling about how things went. I'll start by saying...

13.
Final Thoughts

"Out beyond ideas of wrongdoing and rightdoing,
there is a field. I will meet you there."
Jalal al-Din Rumi[27]

In my first year teaching at Skidmore, a student in my criminal justice class was living off campus, and her house was burglarized. She was home asleep, and her three housemates were out. She never heard or saw the offender, but several items were taken. A few nights later, the four friends—all female—were hanging out in their living room and were startled when they saw a man staring through the window, watching them.

Of course, they called the police and their parents. The students were quite frightened, and they began to sleep elsewhere at night—sometimes leaving only one of them alone who had not made other plans. Their self-protective efforts were not well-coordinated. The lock on the front door was broken, and they were having trouble getting a response from the landlord to fix it.

They went to our Dean of Student Affairs, who told them that since they lived off campus, there wasn't anything the college could do for them except refer them to the counseling center. Because they were adults and had chosen to live off campus, it was up to them to take the necessary steps to protect themselves and negotiate with the landlord.

At this point, they all wanted to move out and to renegotiate the lease. The dean said that the offender, who had not been caught, was not likely to be another student, so this was really a police matter.

We discussed these responses in class, and all agreed that what the dean said was true, but it didn't seem very helpful. It didn't meet the needs of the students. I asked them what justice required, and their first response was to find the perpetrator. Maybe the police should stake out the place and double their efforts to catch the person. Then he should be put in jail. But, in the absence of an offender, they did not see a way for justice to be achieved.

Because we were reading about restorative justice, I pointed out that our criminal justice system is very offender-centered. All of our energy is devoted to finding criminals and punishing them—the "trail 'em, nail 'em, jail 'em" approach to justice.

Restorative justice is different because it is balanced between its attention to offenders and to victims. It is different because it is a harm-centered approach. The first questions that are asked are different. Instead of "Who did it, and what should we do to him or her?" restorative justice asks, "What is the harm and how can it be repaired?"

Reframing the question in this way, I asked the class again, what could be a just response to our classmate's predicament? This time, the class immediately focused on her needs in the moment. She felt unsafe. She felt trapped in a housing situation that she did not want to be in.

After a period of brain-storming, the class agreed that they wanted to help. They encouraged her to continue working with the landlord to be released from the housing contract. One person in the class said that he knew how to change a lock and if the housemates would pay for the parts, he would come over that day and take care of it.

The group decided that they did not want any of the housemates to spend another night alone in the house and encouraged the student to create a schedule with her roommates so all would know the plans of the others. And they committed to taking turns calling the classmate each night to make sure she was not alone and decided that one of them would go over and spend the night if she was.

These students found creative and meaningful solutions for their fellow classmate and crime victim. It was also a learning opportunity for them to refocus their attention from offender to victim and from punishment to community building. In that field beyond wrongdoing and "rightdoing," they found a new kind of justice that involved them in a creative problem-solving process, actively engaged their participation, taught them how to apply their generosity and good will, and enabled them to offer real, practical assistance to a friend in need.

I frequently ask student conduct administrators if their office has a mission that includes helping harmed parties even when the offender has not been identified. Few say yes. Restorative justice offers student conduct programs a disciplinary response that is frequently a transformative learning opportunity for all students, whether they have caused harm or been affected by it. Restorative justice offers a hopeful and empowering response to misconduct and a chance to rethink the overly legalistic approaches that now dominate the field of student conduct administration.

Endnotes

1 An earlier version of this case study appeared in *Student Affairs eNews*, December 20, 2011.

2 Melton, Ada Pecos. "Indigenous Justice Systems and Tribal Society," in *Judicature* 79 (1995):126-133.

3 Bazemore, Gordon. "Restorative Justice and Earned Redemption," in *American Behavioral Scientist* 41 (1998):768-813.

4 Braithwaite, John and Declan Roche. "Responsibility and Restorative Justice," in *Restorative Community Justice: Repairing Harm and Transforming Communities*, edited by Gordon Bazemore and Mara Schiff (Cincinnati, OH: Anderson, 2001), 63-84.

5 Akchurin, Roane, Joyce Ester, Pricilla Mori, and Amy Van Meter. "Conferencing Case Study: The Lounge, Leg Hair, and Learning," in *Restorative Justice on the College Campus: Promoting Student Growth and Responsibility, and Reawakening the Spirit of Campus Community*, edited by David R. Karp and Thom Allena (Springfield, IL: Charles C Thomas, 2004), 70-76.

6 Pavela, Gary. "Limiting the 'Pursuit of Perfect Justice' on Campus: A Proposed Code of Student Conduct," in *The Journal of College and University Law* 6 (1979-1980):137-160.

[7] Stoner, Edward N. and John W. Lowery. "Navigating Past the 'Spirit of Insubordination': A Twenty-First Century Model Student Conduct Code with a Model Hearing Script," in *Journal of College and University Law* 31 (2004):1-77.

[8] Dean, Laura A. *CAS Professional Standards for Higher Education,* 7th edition (Washington, D.C.: Council for the Advancement of Standards in Higher Education, 2009), 359.

[9] Pavela, Gary. *Law and Policy Report* 334, Association for Student Conduct Administration, October 1, 2009.

[10] Braithwaite, John. *Restorative Justice and Responsive Regulation* (New York: Oxford University Press, 2002).

[11] For an extended analysis of differences between a restorative justice conference and a model code hearing, see David R. Karp, "Reading the Scripts: The Restorative Justice Conference and the Student Conduct Hearing Board," in *Reframing Campus Conflict: Student Conduct Process through a Social Justice Lens,* edited by Jennifer Meyer Schrage and Nancy Geist Giacomini (Sterling, VA: Stylus Publishers, 2009), 155-174.

[12] Maloney, Dennis. *Tributary Streams of a Healing River: An In Depth Study of Restorative Justice, 10 DVD Collection* (Heartspeak Productions, 2007), available at http://www.heartspeakproductions.ca/tributary-streams-of-a-healing.

[13] Jelinek, Libby. "Program to Revamp Student Justice," in *The Vista,* October 13, 2011, available at http://www.theusdvista.com/news/program-to-revamp-student-justice-1.2647643?pagereq=1.

[14] Conversation with the author.

[15] Wachtel, Joshua. "Healing After a Student Suicide: Restorative Circles at the University of Vermont," in *Restorative Practices E-Forum*, February 12, 2011, available at http://www.iirp.edu/article_detail. php?article_id=Njg4.

[16] Pranis, Kay, Barry Stuart, and Mark Wedge. *Peacemaking Circles* (St. Paul, MN: Living Justice Press, 2003), 70.

[17] Conversation with the author.

[18] This case was described to me by Stacy Vander Velde, Associate Director, Office of Student Conflict Resolution, University of Michigan.

[19] Ross, Rupert. *Returning to the Teachings: Exploring Aboriginal Justice* (New York: Penguin, 1996), 175.

[20] Conversation with the author.

[21] For an elaboration of STARR Project research findings, see Karp and Sacks, "Research Findings on Restorative Justice and Alcohol Violations," and Karp and Sacks, "Student Conduct, Restorative Justice, and Student Development."

[22] The data show mean satisfaction scores for 135 restorative justice cases.

[23] Each dimension was constructed by multiple indicators.

[24] Mok, Harry. "UC Explores Restorative Justice in Improving Campus Climate," in *UC Newsroom*, January 27, 2012, available at http://www.universityofcalifornia. edu/news/article/27045.

[25] Conversation with the author.

[26] This script is based on conferencing scripts by Sandy Bowles, Guilford College; Chris Dinnan, Vermont Department of Corrections; Charles Barton, *Restorative Justice: The Empowerment Model*; and Terry O'Connell et al., *Conferencing Handbook: The New Real Justice Training Manual*.

[27] Rumi, Jalal al-Din. *The Essential Rumi*, Coleman Barks, translator (New York: HarperOne, 2004).

Resources

Website: www.CampusRJ.com

A website that provides general resources for campus restorative justice, including links to publications and campus programs.

David Karp's publications focusing on campus restorative justice

Karp, David R. and Thom Allena, eds. *Restorative Justice on the College Campus: Promoting Student Growth and Responsibility, and Reawakening the Spirit of Campus Community* (Springfield, IL: Charles C Thomas, 2004).

Karp, David R. "Campus Justice is Behind the Times," in *Inside Higher Ed* October 28, 2005.

Karp, David R. and Suzanne Conrad. "Restorative Justice and College Student Misconduct," in *Public Organization Review* 5 (2005):315-333.

Karp, David R. "Not with a Bang but a Whimper: A Missed Opportunity for Restorative Justice in a Plagiarism Case," in *Journal of Student Conduct Administration* 2(1) (2009):26-30.

Karp, David R. "Reading the Scripts: The restorative Justice Conference and the Student Conduct hearing Board," in *Reframing Campus Conflict: Student Conduct Process through a Social Justice Lens.* Edited by Jennifer Meyer Schrage and Nancy Geist Giacomini (Sterling, VA: Stylus, 2009).

Karp, David R. "Spirit Horse and the Principles of Restorative Justice," in *Student Affairs eNews* December 20, 2011.

Karp, David R. and Casey Sacks. "Research Findings on Restorative Justice and Alcohol Violations," in *NASPA Alcohol and Other Drug Knowledge Community Newsletter* Fall 2012.

Karp, David R. and Casey Sacks. "Student Conduct, Restorative Justice, and Student Development: Findings from the STARR Project (Student Accountability and Restorative Research Project)," in *Contemporary Justice Review* Forthcoming 2013.

Restorative justice books in the Little Books of Justice and Peacebuilding series

Lederach, John Paul. *The Little Book of Conflict Transformation* (Intercourse, PA: Good Books, 2003).

MacRae, Allan and Howard Zehr. *The Little Book of Family Group Conferences, New Zealand Style* (Intercourse, PA: Good Books, 2004).

Pranis, Kay. *The Little Book of Circle Processes* (Intercourse, PA: Good Books, 2005).

Stutzman Amstutz, Lorraine. *The Little Book of Victim Offender Conferencing* (Intercourse, PA: Good Books, 2009).

Stutzman Amstutz, Lorraine and Judy H. Mullet. *The Little Book of Restorative Discipline for Schools* (Intercourse, PA: Good Books, 2005).

Toews, Barbara. *The Little Book of Restorative Justice for People in Prison* (Intercourse, PA: Good Books, 2006).

Zehr, Howard. *The Little Book of Restorative Justice* (Intercourse, PA: Good Books, 2002).

Other important restorative justice books

Boyes-Watson, Carolyn. *Peacemaking Circles and Urban Youth* (St. Paul, MN: Living Justice Press, 2008).

Braithwaite, John. *Restorative Justice and Responsive Regulation* (New York: Oxford University Press, 2002).

Liebmann, Marian. *Restorative Justice: How it Works* (London and Philadelphia: Jessica Kingsley Publishers, 2007).

Pranis, Kay, Barry Stuart, and Mark Wedge. *Peacemaking Circles* (St. Paul, MN: Living Justice Press, 2003).

Ross, Rupert. *Returning to the Teachings: Exploring Aboriginal Justice* (New York: Penguin, 1996).

Schrage, Jennifer Meyer and Nancy Geist Giacomini, eds. *Reframing Campus Conflict: Student Conduct Process through a Social Justice Lens* (Sterling, VA: Stylus, 2009).

Umbreit, Mark and Marilyn Peterson Armour. *Restorative Justice Dialogues: A Research-Based Approach to Working with Victims, Offenders, Families, and Communities* (New York: Springer, 2010).

Wallis, Pete and Barbara Tudor. *The Pocket Guide to Restorative Justice* (London and Philadelphia: Jessica Kingsley Publishers, 2008).

Zehr, Howard. *Change Lenses* (Scottdale, PA: Herald Press, 1990).

About the Author

David R. Karp is Associate Dean of Student Affairs and Professor of Sociology at Skidmore College in Saratoga Springs, New York. His scholarship focuses on restorative justice in community and campus settings and on prison programs preparing inmates for return to the community. David has published six books and more than 100 academic papers. He was the recipient of the 2010 Donald D. Gehring Award from the Association for Student Conduct Administration. David received a B.A. in Peace and Conflict Studies from the University of California at Berkeley and a Ph.D. in Sociology from the University of Washington.

METHOD OF PAYMENT

❏ Check or Money Order
*(payable to **Good Books** in U.S. funds)*

❏ Please charge my:

    ❏ MasterCard   ❏ Visa

    ❏ Discover   ❏ American Express

\# _____

exp. date _____

Signature _____

Name _____

Address _____

City _____

State _____

Zip _____

Phone _____

Email _____

SHIP TO: (if different)

Name _____

Address _____

City _____

State _____

Zip _____

Mail order to: **Good Books**
P.O. Box 419 • Intercourse, PA 17534-0419
Call toll-free: 800/762-7171
Fax toll-free: 888/768-3433
Prices subject to change.

Group Discounts for

The Little Book of Restorative Justice for Colleges and Universities
ORDER FORM

If you would like to order multiple copies of
**The Little Book of Restorative Justice for Colleges
and Universities** by David R. Karp for groups you
know or are a part of, use this form. (Discounts
apply only for more than one copy.)
Photocopy this page as often as you like.

The following discounts apply:

1 copy	$4.95
2-5 copies	$4.45 each (a 10% discount)
6-10 copies	$4.20 each (a 15% discount)
11-20 copies	$3.96 each (a 20% discount)
21-99 copies	$3.45 each (a 30% discount)
100 or more	$2.97 each (a 40% discount)

Free Shipping for orders of 100 or more!
Prices subject to change.

Quantity   *Price*   *Total*

_____ copies of **Restorative Justice for Col/Uni** @ _____ _____

Shipping & Handling
(U.S. orders only: add 10%; $3.95 minimum) _____
For international orders, please call 800/762-7171, ext. 221

PA residents add 6% sales tax _____

TOTAL _____

800/762-7171 • www.GoodBooks.com